PUPPIES TO COLOR

have fun learning a little about these cute little dogs and also coloring them

MAX G R

CHIHUAHUA

The small breed dog par excellence is the Chihuahua. It is the smallest dog in the world, and also the longest living (it can live 20 years). Its tiny size contrasts with its brave and energetic character. It is a playful animal and is devoted to its owners. In addition to a lot of love and care, we must keep in mind that the Chihuahua is originally from Mexico, so it does not tolerate the cold well, so it cannot lack blankets in winter. There are 6 types of Chihuahua and all of them are types of dogs that do not grow. And as for colors, there are several to choose from.

CHIHUAHUA

MINIATURE TERRIER

As their name suggests, these dogs combine the qualities of a terrier and a miniature, although the latter's characteristics soon took the lead in the breeding program. These dogs were once used to kill rats by the dozen, so they are alert and never overly nervous.

These adorable little dogs are fun and fit into any home environment. Their terrier influences make them a curious and energetic breed, but they are happy to spend the day at home with their human family.

MINIATURE TERRIER

BULL TERRIER

Disciplined and gentle, Bull Terriers are especially good with people and are well suited as family companions.

Robust, well balanced and active, Bull Terriers have a lively, stubborn and intelligent expression. In action, Bull Terriers look well-groomed and move with regular, carefree and simple strides, with characteristic agility.

BULL TERRIER

CARLINO

A popular member of the toy breed group, the pug is canine fun that comes in a barrel-shaped package. With their unique appearance, they are always the star of the show and also have a sweet and playful disposition. They also have an easy-to-maintain coat, don't require a lot of exercise, and aren't a breed that barks much either. The pug has its own Latin motto, "Multum in Parvo," which simply means, "Much in a little."

CARLINO

TECKEL

It's no exaggeration to say that the Standard Longhaired Dachshund is dogged in its pursuit of all things: part of the bloodhound group, the breed is highly valued for its compact size. You may be wondering how such a small dog can catch something. But the Dachshund was bred small for sport, specifically to bury itself in narrow dirt passages and find badgers and smaller animals. With these wickers, it is not surprising that the result was a brave and "takes no prisoners" dog. As if their single size wasn't enough, Dachshunds also come in a miniature version.

TECKEL

ENGLISH BULLDOG

The English Bulldog is a medium-sized breed that has a fairly extensive and characteristic build. The large head it has gives it a somewhat imposing appearance, which has nothing to do with its true character. This one has small, drooping ears, and a snout where you can see a characteristic wrinkle of skin located between the eyes and its nose. The organs that give the animal vision have a dark color and remain quite open, although the abundant skin that the animal has on its face covers them to a small percentage. One of the key physical characteristics of the English Bulldog is its large, drooping upper lips that give this breed "an unfriendly face."

ENGLISH BULLDOG

DOBERMAN

With a rectangular trunk and a fairly rigid position, the Doberman is a dog that stands out for its evident muscular definition. Although it is not one of the largest dogs that exists, the body of this breed demonstrates clear physical strength. The legs of this dog are thin but resistant and the tail is long and narrow. The head of this dog is long and thin, composed of brown eyes and a medium-sized nose. The ears of this dog used to be trimmed by its owners, causing a sharp shape and a tense position of the ears. With the fortunate prohibition on cropping dogs' ears, the Doberman's ears are large and remain drooping on the animal's face.

DOBERMAN

STAFFORDSHIRE BULL TERRIER

The Staffordshire Bull Terrier has a rough, muscular appearance that is very common in sister breeds such as the Pit Bull Terrier. Its size, unlike other similar dogs, is medium and adopts a clear square shape. Its tense and widened chest stands out, its well arched ribs, its thick chest and the fibrous legs that support the broad trunk. The head of this dog stands out for the evident breadth of its skull and its overwhelming size. This area is also not spared from the remarkable musculature, especially in the animal's jaws. The medium and dark eyes of this breed result in an intense look that is usually accompanied by the constant panting shown by the dog's wide mouth. And what can we say about their ears? They clearly have a small size compared to the size of the head and usually remain semi-erect.

STAFFORDSHIRE BULL TERRIER

COCKER SPANIEL INGLES

The English Cocker Spaniel is a dog that stands out for the enormous intelligence it has, the main reason why the training of this dog is faster and more effective. But this must be taught from puppy age, if not, behavioral problems are very likely!

The affection that he gives to all the members of his family is unmistakable and he always has patience when dealing with the little ones in the house. It is a very active breed that will always want to leave the house and greatly appreciates being near swamps, rivers or lagoons, since it is a great swimmer.

However, the English Cocker Spaniel is a dog that adapts perfectly to life in the city. In addition, they will not object to sharing a flat with other dogs, since they are a breed that is quite respectful of others.

COCKER SPANIEL INGLES

SIBERIAN HUSKY

The Siberian Husky, also known as the Siberian Wolf, is one of the most intelligent dogs that exist, so they are dogs that assimilate commands much more quickly – without forgetting that in certain behaviors they are somewhat stubborn.

It is a somewhat colder and more independent dog than others, although it does not stop showing its love to its loved ones.

Living with a Siberian Husky usually does not cause problems, since they have a fairly calm behavior and are usually friendly with other pets that live in the same four walls.

If there is something notable about the behavior of the Siberian Husky, it is that it does not usually bark, it is a dog that howls!

SIBERIAN HUSKY

BELGIAN SHEPHERD

There are four varieties: Groenendael, Laekenois, Belgian Malinois, Tervueren, In general, the four varieties of Belgian Shepherd have similar behavior between them. These are dogs that are always on alert, enriching their undeniable guardianship work.

He stands out for his very strong attachment to his master and it is not strange that he acts firmly and barks at people he does not know, especially the Belgian Malinois, which has a more aggressive character than the other three varieties. These are somewhat calmer and, historically, have had a more pastoral func

BELGIAN SHEPHERD

NEWFOUNDLAND DOG

It's impossible for this dog's physique not to remind you of a bear! The Newfoundland has a fairly long and thick body from which four wide and muscular legs emerge, and a thick and long tail that allows it to be a magnificent swimmer. The ribs, trunk and belly of the animal are large, as is the head. In the latter, the Newfoundland has small eyes that are usually dark in color, small, drooping ears that have a triangular shape and a large snout.

The dog's nose will be a different color depending on the pigmentation of its long coat: black, white or brown. This hair is made up of a double layer that protects the breed's skin from possible pathogens that water can cause.

NEWFOUNDLAND DOG

SAINT BERNARD

It is one of the largest dogs that exist, with a voluminous head that supports large floppy ears. The Saint Bernard is a fairly calm dog, showing a sweetness and affection that contrasts with its enormous appearance. It is one of the dogs that makes education the easiest, since its tremendous intelligence allows it to learn all the instructions quickly.

He is a perfect guard dog that will always ensure the safety of his family, in which he has his favorite members: the children. When it comes to playing, the Saint Bernard is one more and shows the tremendous love he has for the little ones in the house.

It is not a breed that is at all conflictive with other dogs, and will rarely be aggressive. He is one of the most peaceful dogs out there!

SAINT BERNARD

GERMAN DOG OR GREAT DANE

Without a doubt, the German Dogo is one of the largest dog breeds in the world. Everything that is great about the German Dogo is calm and affectionate. He has a unique temperance and knows how to perfectly detect the mood of his owners. He demonstrates a special bond with his family and has an exclusive relationship with the little ones in the house.

This is a dog that will bark only when someone strange approaches, a characteristic that makes it an excellent guard dog. He does not usually confront other dogs and will only be aggressive if there are reasons for it. Learning it is effective, although sometimes it can be more expensive than usual. However, with patience the German Doge assimilates everything his owner teaches him!

GERMAN DOG OR GREAT DANE

GOLDEN RETRIEVER

Kindness, affection and intelligence are the three words that best define this dog. The Golden Retriever is one of the nicest and most tender dogs that exist. He is always willing to play with the little ones in the house and is a dog that does not seek conflicts with other dogs.

This calmness and passivity of the Golden Retriever makes it impossible for this dog to not be ideal to act as a guardian of the home. However, his calm attitude allows him to be one of the races most willing to assimilate orders. This, added to his enormous intelligence, makes training him a simple task.

GOLDEN RETRIEVER

AIREDALE TERRIER

In general, the Airedale Terrier is a very happy dog that shows unconditional affection for its family. Although he transmits a special affinity with children, it is dangerous to leave him alone with them, since he is a rather rough dog. However, this breed is an excellent protector of the home and is always willing to stand up for its loved ones.

The education of the Airedale Terrier must be clear from its puppy stage, a time in which the dog is most impatient and impulsive. Thanks to his correct training - which is not an easy task - we will achieve a better coexistence with him, removing possible destructive behaviors.

Socialization is also a point to take into account in its first months of life, since by accustoming the dog to direct contact with other dogs and humans, we will ensure that in adulthood it is a less territorial dog and accepts sharing moments with other dogs.

AIREDALE TERRIER

I hope you had fun coloring these dogs, and at the same time that you learned about them.
There are many other breeds of dogs to learn a lot about, and I'm sure you have one of them at home, find out what breed it is and what its characteristics are to get to know it better.
See you soon and leave me a nice review atte...your friend
MAX G R.